Fire!

To O. John
—C.G.

First published in paperback in 2008

Published in Canada by Fitzhenry & Whiteside, 195 Allstate Parkway, Markham, Ontario L3R 4T8
Published in the United States by Fitzhenry & Whiteside, 311 Washington Street, Brighton, Massachusetts 02135

www.fitzhenry.ca   godwit@fitzhenry.ca

10 9 8 7 6 5 4 3 2

Library and Archives Canada Cataloguing in Publication

Godkin, Celia
Fire / Celia Godkin.

Reading grade level: 2-4
Interest age level: 6-9
ISBN 978-1-55455-082-1 (pbk.).   ISBN 1-55041-889-0 (bound)

1. Fire ecology—Juvenile literature. 2. Forest fires—Juvenile literature. 3. Forest
ecology—Juvenile literature. 1. Écologie des feux—Ouvrages pour la jeunesse. 2. Forêts—Incendies-
Ouvrages pour la jeunesse. 3. Écologie forestière—Ouvrages pour la jeunesse. I. Title.

QH545.F5G63 2006   j577.2'4 C2005-907260-1   QH545*

U.S. Publisher Cataloging-in-Publication Data
(Library of Congress Standards)

Godkin, Celia.
Fire! / Celia Godkin.
[32] p. : col. ill. ;   cm.
Summary: The life cycle of a forest is examined, from its devastation to its gradual renewal.
ISBN: 1-55041-889-0 (2006 ed.)   ISBN: 978-1-55455-082-1 (pbk.)
1. Forest fires — Juvenile literature. 2. Forest ecology — Juvenile literature. I. Title.
634.9/618 dc22   SD421.23.G635 2008

Fitzhenry & Whiteside acknowledges with thanks the Canada Council for the Arts,
and the Ontario Arts Council for their support of our publishing program.
We acknowledge the financial support of the Government of Canada
through the Book Publishing Industry Development Program (BPIDP) for our publishing activities.

Design by Wycliffe Smith Designs Inc.

Printed in Hong Kong, China

Fire!

Celia Godkin

Fitzhenry & Whiteside

It was another hot day
in the forest.
Not a leaf stirred.
Not a breeze whispered.
All was quiet and still.

High in the treetops
a hawk waited silently.
Down in the shadows
a deer nibbled greenery.
Deep in a burrow
a mouse nursed her little ones.

deer mouse

Here and there in the forest
were clearings
where old trees had died and fallen,
brought down by wind and storm.

Though it was hot
in the shady forest,
it was hotter still
in the sunny clearings.

cedar waxwing, snowshoe hare

It hadn't rained in many weeks.
Everything was dry and scorched.
Every day the sun beat down,
out of a cloudless sky.

In the clearings the small plants,
which had once been
green and juicy,
had shriveled and dried.
They were now
brown and crisp.

red admiral butterfly

bumble bee

two-spot ladybug

grasshopper

Late in the afternoon
a hot wind began to blow.
Storm clouds gathered.
Lightning snapped and crackled,
but no rain came.

A bolt of lightning
shot from the sky
and hit a tall tree
beside a clearing.

spruce, aspen, and pine trees

The lightning shot down the tree
to the kindling-dry leaves below.
Sparks flew.
The leaves burst into flame.
Soon the clearing was ablaze.

The fire swept across the clearing
and spread to the trees.
Now the forest was ablaze.

white-tailed deer

The hawk flew up and away.
The deer ran for her life.
The mouse hid deep in her burrow,
where the fire could not reach her
or her little ones.

The fire raged for many days.
Many trees were burned,
but most of the animals escaped.

red-tailed hawk

Then, one day,
black rain clouds blew over
the smoke-darkened sky.
Raindrops hissed and spattered
on the hot embers.

The rain poured down,
soaking the burning forest.
Slowly the fire died down
and fizzled out.

open and closed cones

After many days of rain,
the ground was a soggy mess
of charred timber.

It looked like nothing
would ever grow there again.

pine seeds sprouting

But after a week or two,
little green shoots
began to poke through the soil.

Some plants grew
from underground roots.
Other plants grew from seeds
that survived
the heat of the fire
or from seeds
blown in by the wind.

fireweed, dandelion, aspen seeds

Soon the whole area
of burnt-out forest
was a bright carpet of color.

Deer wandered back
to nibble on the fresh green shoots.
Mice scurried by,
searching for good things to eat.
Hawks flew over,
looking for mice.

fireweed

After a while
some of the plants
with woody stems
grew taller than the rest.

In time,
they became the trees
of the new forest.
In time, the new forest
began to look
just like the old forest.

spruce grouse

It was another hot day
in the forest.
Not a leaf stirred.
Not a breeze whispered.
All was quiet and still.

red squirrel, pileated woodpecker

VIEW OF A WILDERNESS FOREST

In areas where summers are dry, fire is a natural force that helps keep the forest healthy.
Fire causes changes that reveal a patchwork of different habitats for many kinds of plants and animals.

OLD FOREST
When a forest is a few hundred years old, trees begin
to die. The dead trees are blown down in storms,
creating sunny patches where grasses, wildflowers,
and shrubs can grow, as well as new saplings
(young trees). If the forest is in a wet area, the fallen
trees decompose; but if the forest is in a dry area, the
dead trees, branches, and leaves pile up on the forest
floor, forming fuel that readily ignites when sparked by
lightning, campfires, or cigarettes.

THE LINE between young and old forest marks the boundary of an earlier fire.

YOUNG FORESTS act as natural firebreaks.

YOUNG FOREST
A few years after a fire, the trees have grown taller
than the other plants. The area is densely packed
with young trees, creating shade where smaller plants
will not grow. There is little dead plant material to
provide fuel, so fires rarely start in young forests.

CHARRED REMAINS
After a big fire, the land is charred and black, but
minerals that were once locked in the plants have been
released as ash into the soil. The enriched soil is
ideal for new plant growth.

RIVERS
and roads may act as firebreaks.

LIGHTNING
Lightning will hit a forest many times each season, but it will only spark a fire when the forest is very dry.

FOREST FIRE
Most fires burn out quickly. Large fires occur most often in old forests, where there is plenty of fuel in the form of dead trees and dry leaves and branches.

CAMPERS
Some fires are started by people who don't properly extinguish their campfires or toss cigarette butts on the ground.

SNAGS
are burnt trees still standing after a fire.

NEW GROWTH
Just a few weeks after a fire, plants will sprout in the burnt-out areas, which will soon become a carpet of lush new growth. The new growth will include grasses, wildflowers, shrubs, and saplings.

HOW LIFE RETURNS
TO A FOREST AFTER A FIRE

Black Bear

White-tailed Deer

Coyote

Pileated Woodpecker

LARGE ANIMALS can usually outrun a fire. Once the plants begin to grow back, larger animals, attracted by the lush new growth, will return. Predators soon follow their prey animals.

BIRDS easily escape fires by flying away from them. After a fire, snags provide good nesting sites for birds like woodpeckers; but birds that prefer the forest habitat will remain in areas that have not been cleared by fire.

Fireweed

Deer Mouse

SMALL ANIMALS survive fires by hiding in underground burrows. Pine seeds released by the heat of the fire provide a plentiful food source for many small animals after the ground has cooled.

UNDERGROUND ROOTS AND STEMS
Grasses, wildflowers, and shrubs will burn in a fire; but their underground roots usually survive, and the plants quickly sprout again.

GROUNDHOGS
Animals like groundhogs, which prefer forest edges, will move into areas recovering from fire. Their tree-dwelling relatives, the squirrels, will return only when the trees grow back.

WIND-BORNE SEEDS are blown into burnt-out areas, where they thrive in the fertile soil. Plants with wind-borne seeds include all the grasses, many wildflowers, and trees like aspen and birch.

Aspen Seeds

Dandelion Seeds

Fireweed Seeds

ASPEN
After a fire, many small aspen trees will sprout from a single large root system that has survived the fire.

Cedar Waxwing

Aspen Seedlings

EVERGREEN TREES (PINE, SPRUCE, FIR)
Some evergreen trees drop their lower branches so future fires cannot travel up the trees from the ground. Should the fire start in a clearing, however, the bushes and young trees provide a ladder that the fire can climb to reach the branches.

Bearberry Bush

Pine Seedlings

BERRIES
A variety of wild bushes produce berries, which are eaten by many animals. The seeds in the berries pass through the gut unharmed. When dropped in an area cleared by fire, these seeds will sprout into new plants.

Pine Cone

PINE CONES
Pine trees produce two kinds of pine cones, both of which contain seeds. One kind opens to release its seeds in normal conditions; the other kind is sealed tight with a thick coat of resin. It takes the heat of a forest fire to melt the resin and release the seeds.

AUTHOR'S NOTE

Every year, thousands of forest fires burn across North America. Though we must protect people and their homes from forest fires, we need not be concerned about the effect of fires on the forests themselves. Fires have been occurring for thousands of years; for many forests, fire is as essential as rain. In the boreal forest, where this story takes place, fires actually help the forest stay healthy.

Fires release the mineral nutrients that are locked in old trees by turning them into ash. The ash helps make a rich soil that allows new plants to grow. Without fires, many forests would lose their capacity to renew themselves. Without fires, there would be fewer plant and animal species in North America.

To find out more about forest fires, check these websites:
www.enviroliteracy.org/article.php/46.html
www.infoplease.com/spot/forestfire1.html
fire.cfs.nrcan.gc.ca/index_e.php

And especially for teachers:
school.discovery.com/lessonplans/programs/forestfires/